HYDROPONICS FOR BEGINNERS:

Discover the Advantages of Hydroponics &
How to Develop an Unexpensive Solid System with
The Right Knowledge and Suitable Materials.
Build Your Healthy Garden Now!
(Part 2)

by **EMILY BATES**

Table Of Contents

PART 2

CHAPTER 1:

Hydroponics Gardening Soil Report

It is essential to know what exactly is the difference between the two. There are some crucial points that we all know that hydroponic garden uses water and garden use the ground floor as a base material for fruit and vegetable cultivation. But other smaller things should be considered so that the best option to select.

In many people's minds, a question that can come when all things are the most critical needs of the plants, so why do we need a way to grow a plant. Different people have different answers to this question. Some say the media as support on the ground in the release of gases and facilitates absorption or installation requires means root anchorage and physical consistency maintain. Here in this chapter, we will learn about the two methods of culture, play media, and see which one is best for you, the environment, and the plant itself.

Hydroponics It is a technique to grow and use to develop plants without soil. In this system, the plants will grow and improve their development in a process that includes a solution that is rich in nutrients instead of soil beds. The hydroponic cultivation method is known as landless agriculture. In this type of gardening, rather than soil, hydroponic gardening is a bit expensive, since in this process necessary special tools used water-based. You must also be a source of artificial light and nutrients with a specific format, which helps to do a better and better performance.

The main objective of soilless gardening growth is to protect the root system of plants and water supply and nutrients and support.

There is more need for working the land is, this method can be used for agriculture in urban areas and where to do on-ground agriculture is not possible. Hydroponic media and nutrient loss grow, is much lower in these are dictated in this area. Moreover, this process is very environmentally friendly and less polluting.

Performance in this garden is high, and the harvest is also very easy.

About hydroponic garden

"In this garden, there is less use of labor

-The plants grow faster than the bed to the floor, and there is no need for weeding

-The plants and crops can throughout the year, be grown indoors and outdoors

-In this method, it is less use of potted plants

-Use of pesticides is minimal and contributes to the reduction of Disease

Soil Gardening

It is a process to produce plants with soil., Which means that the media here is the ground. The land is mixed on an excellent planting with other ingredients. The earth is a mixture of many things, such as gases, liquids, minerals, and many other organisms as well. It is the oldest type of planting; It is also that the surface layer of the soil is known. It is used in plantations in the open. It is not because it is unhealthy roots inside. It is one of the cheapest methods on the farm.

Today there are many ways for soil gardening. People can have space in the garden fruits and vegetables increase in a small area where there is good sunlight, and precipitation may be in the garden soil if one was growing on the cultivation of the earth, which can be divided into two subcategories on the ground and growing in pots. In the field of culture, the country is prepared with many other pre-culture exercises first. There are a few years; people do not use fertilizers. You are more likely used for crop rotation to maintain soil fertility. But currently, people do not change the system was so much space. Therefore, for more yield, farmers fertilizer uses on their fields. It is one of the ways to make the fertile soil and plants absorb these nutrients.

The plug is usually used for export or in horticulture. The media, which is inserted in the box, depends on the harvest.

On the landscaped site development

sol gardening helps to reduce air pollution and create a healthy environment

It gives me the planting teamwork less healthy and less investment

It helps a high capacity of water retention, reduce water wastage

Garden help feed people and animals -SOL

The difference between garden soil and hydroponic garden

to put Hydroponic using relatively few nutrients materials in plants relative to the ground gardening. The reason for this is that there are nutrients in the standalone environment that can easily control waste.

Best of hydroponics is that there is very little fertilizer used in it, compared to the traditional farmland. in the flowing water and the quality of the water damaged There are a lot of fertilizer by the people and two animals used

Another critical difference is that the hydroponic method is easy to grow and more then yields to the floor

When we speak of space, hydroponic takes very little space compared to the cultivation of the soil. If a plant growing in the ground is required to move a lot of space. But in hydroponics, it is immersed in water with an oxygenated nutrient solution, any time your plants with perfectly calibrated nutrients.

Another advantage of the environment, the hydroponics is to use less water about the floor gardening, that water is supplied to the plants in a fixed ratio. It is preferred that the water recycled in it. However, to till the soil, water is wasted and recycled. A portion of the dripping water from the tank bottom is on the ground, and a part of the evaporated water on the floor. The hydroponic farming advantage for the farmer added that the cost is reduced to water, which means that production costs reduced. Therefore, plant roots absorb water is needed and leave the rest.

In hydroponics, it means you have full control over the harvest, that he is the owner of the crop. You must make full control over the factors you a healthy life of a plant, such as light, space, moisture, nutrient content, and mix. During must gardening in the soil depend on many uncontrollable factors such as sunlight and rain

No weed problem in hydroponics. If you had a large farm, you know how difficult it is, the weeds must be taken off the top of the beds. And a long way.

Moreover, the need is to broaden the agricultural air through it in the cultivation of the soil. But in hydroponics, it is necessary to pour a little water in perlite and ready. It is convenient and saves time

They are less hydroponic on the floor of traditional culture because of the above reasons, parasites, and diseases. In hydroponics, the soil is removed and replaced with a means for hydroponics. Therefore, transmitted by the soil-borne conditions are eliminated, and garden soil insects that infest

hydroponic gardeners are easy to make, even at strategic locations, which means that culture is grown as well as near the market area. This means that you also reduce transportation costs, which ultimately reduce the cost of production. Hence, you earn more profit. But this is not the case with soil in the garden. cannot grow crops where you have the land and the cost of transportation, it also tends to be high tended

Hydroponics works well and is easy to configure. It is possible to grow plants in each yard of the house. This concept of urban gardening can remove all your worries on the food security of society.

On the other hand, he has no control over the food you get ground gardening, and you can keep no control over how it is grown

Hydroponics provides the plant in need of a precise amount, which means that the plant will grow faster, compared to the cultivation of the soil. Not only do the plants hydroponically are healthier adults.

Thus, at the end of this chapter, hydroponics is the best tillage. In the next, we will explain how to choose the best hydroponic system to your needs and preferences.

CHAPTER 2:

How to build system Hydroponics

How to build a homemade hydroponic system

To develop various methods, such as a hydroponic system, have already registered with different types of hydroponic systems. Likewise, there are different ways to deal with mounting a measure hydroponic system, the various strategies, and approaches, including.

It consists of growing plants in hydroponic water and nutrient availability used without dirt. Hydroponic gardens are a little less challenging to improve continually to start at home for you. There is a wide range of styles that can be mounted by gardens, the wick systems to be the most popular deep-water cultures and methods of nutrient film. With simple, you can create a home garden in any case.

Process 1

Create a pure system Wick

Turn 1. Main 4 (10 cm) on a plastic pot. Reuse a half-empty US Lady (1.9 L) bottle of soda. Just use start with a pair of scissors or a knife, the name of the container, about 4 inches (10 cm) from the tip. Cutting completely evacuated through the box until the top.

• A soft drink with the starter 1 will ground. You, when the possibility of what you need 10 or fewer plants in the hydroponic garden shed should, with a lady of the United States 20 (76 L) plastic bag.

2. Insert a screwdriver an opening through the glass above. Set the upper pot on a hard surface, such as a cutting board. Keep the top of the sides with the non-dominant hand, while in the middle with a screwdriver punching. Make the opening of about 1/4 inch (0.64 cm) full.

• The screwdriver head on a bright fire degree to soften the plastic cover on the off chance that you have trouble piercing through.

• If a plastic bag to be used to connect to an area along with the protection of the center drill to 3-4 lagoons cutting.

3. Food string through the hole at the top. Cut to a piece of string with a pair of scissors, and it is for about 12 inches (30 cm). The feeding of the final rope through the highest point of the upper part of the container until it is about 6 inches (15 cm) on each side. When the wire at the top is the screw in the pot.

• If you use a large down payment, you can use a little thick rope wick more water to be sent.

Fill the pot base 4 with nutrient supply. Visit your local garden store involved to find a mix of nutrients for hydroponic gardening. You can use a similar provision to pay little attention to what planted in your system. Fill the pan with its base of about 4 C (950 ml) of tap water. Follow discover the camp in their response to nutrient the amount that you must mix in water. If you contain the right amount, mix with a stick mix the water.

• Use locally purchased clean water in your title if you have a hard water tap.

• If you cannot find a blend of nutrients come, you request a web container.

5. Set the highest point above the legs of the pot, so that the wire is immersed most. When he combined the supply of nutrients, set the highest point of the container upside down in

the upper left side. Make sure that it is (2.5 cm) of wire between the top end of the container and the highest points of the arrangement about 1 inch.

• If you use a plastic bag, use a plastic bracket that is (4/3 from 7.6 to 10.2 cm) deep on the protective bag. Make a point of hole openings in the new plastic space so that the alignment with the gaps in her purse.

Place the culture medium and their seeds sixth in the highest point of the container. Find a medium that effectively water and nutrients can go, for example, perlite, coconut fiber, or vermiculite. 2 bunches mean in the upper segment of the pot and gently spreading packaging with the fingers. After the culture medium comprises, the seeds can be planted at a certain depth in the group.

• Every culture medium can be purchased at your local garden house or garden maintenance. All these media work regardless of growth that uses plants.

• The supply of nutrients to the bit in the culture medium of plant food and water to give.

• Wick exceptional work systems for new hydroponic gardeners and non-response cannot build more significant systems. Bit systems are the system that works best for herbs or salad.

Tip: to build plant three seeds in all cases, your successful germination chance. If one more smoking the weakest growth grows than other plants from.

Method 2

The development of a culture system in deep water

1. Turn on the vacuum in the upper part of an espresso plastic carrier like a network size pot. Net pots have so that that water can pass through them without far-fetched flow spaces. Follow the bottom of the pot network on the door over the espresso with a pen or marker. Use of a journal or utility knife for opening estimation cutting, so that the pot engages hermetically in the pattern region. Keep side to shave the edge of the network pot is at the highest level of the cover.

• A coffee supports a plant may contain. If you need to make a bigger hydroponic garden, use a plastic bag with several large pots network.

2. Some X near the edge of the upper part cut of an air tube. Print measure about 1/2 inch (1.3 cm) from the side of the lid and the stain with a pen or marker. Push to make your journal on top of a cut. Rotate 90 degrees cover and another first experience section.

• Your incision in the hole where you put in a cheap meal drinking straw on.

3. Use of 1.4 to 1.2 (0.64 to 1.27 cm) in the culture pipe system in deep water. The X-shaped cut-out determines the finishing cylinder until its anime 6 in (15 cm) attached, or until the bottle reaches the bottom of the compartment. Let upwardly enough tube a bubbling machine to achieve, or from about 1 1/2 feet (46 cm).

4. Enter the seventy-five percent of the Espresso magazine capacity with several nutrients. Nutritious blends are sold in garden stores or online and work each little mixture's attention to pay what is planting. Fill in the seventy-five percent Espresso door of his ability with the tap water. Follow warn the brand categories to mix the perfect measure of the nutrient solution to the water that you use to measure. Use a toothpick to combine mixture with nutrients from the sea. Set Espresso upper rear compartment.

• If hard water from the tap, water purchased refined locally in his field.

Place the culture medium and seeds 5. in the red boat. The next step is to fill the pot until it reaches the upper or coir, perlite, or vermiculite. Sowing the plant seeds on support (1.3 cm) somewhere in their culture medium.

• Go for green or herbal when seeds rather than larger plants sowing.

• All culture media work pays little mind to the type of plant that grows.

• Sowing depth while plants they can change depends on the type of plant - advice with the seed packet to see if they should be planted shallower or more profound.

6. The opposite air bottle with a bubbler and finishing. Dabbling help add oxygen available, so not that their bases asphyxiation. Make sure the surface of your behavior, are between the highest point of the port with the subject in the bubbler and turn-on. Let the bubbly all the time, as the plants grow.

• The supply of nutrients to provide plants with water and the constant food sprayed into the culture medium in his boat, for them to grow.

• Nutrient systems in deep waters are low and easy to support at home. But they do not work admirably for plants that have a long growth period.

• Bubblers can be purchased from your neighborhood pet store or aquarium business.

• Bubblers need to run continuously, or plants could straighten the leg.

Process 3

Using the technique nutrient film

1. A compound of a siphon with an air diffuser at the base of the water tank. Makes an opening 2 (5.1 cm) down from the highest point 20 US (76 L) of a plastic bag with a blade utility. Set the air vents in the bag in a similar lateral supply opening and the air tube through. The entry into the pipe to a pneumatic machine.

• Vents and air traps can at your pet store or aquarium area to be acquired.

2. A submersible water siphon one on the opposite side of the magazine. Set the water trap on the opposite side of the bag as an air diffuser. An opening in the counter-blades is to force 2.3 in (5.1 cm 7.6) from top to bottom and wide enough to accommodate the pipe connection and a half (1.3 cm). Feed cylinder and the power cable through the opening.

• Water siphons can be purchased in your neighborhood pet shop.

3. Fill a large part of the memory with several nutrients. Using about 10 gallons (38 L) of water or flushing valve to totes, so that the siphon and the air diffuser are entirely immersed. Each mixture of nutrients can be used to pay little attention to the plant's growth. Add added nutrient fluid as a target to the water in the bag. Combination arrangement with a mixing rod.

• The nutrient liquid purchased in your garden or neighborhood store on the web.

4. Slope a downpour or a PVC pipe between two stools with the drainage channel. Use 4-6 feet (1.2 to 1.8 m) or the grooves PVC pipe. The addition of a plate 2 x 4 in (5.1 cm x 10.2 cm) on one of the two blocks with screws or nails. Write trestle within 3 feet (0.91 m) away from each other so that their handles only between them and establish or stimulates drain pipe upwards.

• Make sure that the parts of the market, so that the water does not close spreads.

5. openings cut resume their pots in the highest point of the channel. The use of a compound opening saw 3/2 in (5.1 cm to 7.6) for carrying gaps at the highest point of the channel. Wherein each of the plants about 1 foot (30 cm) away from each other to have a space to grow the area for the roots. Spot 1 in each network cup opening as soon as they are cut.

• The channel must be hanging around 4-6 plants depends on how long it is.

• Connections saw holes in your neighborhood business reorganization to be acquired. Make to cut it a point to pick a hollow saw material being.

• The size of the gap is you want to use based on the size of the net pots.

6. At the bottom of the channel and the upper part of the tank can be a channel gap. Drilling a 1 (cm 3.8 2.5) from the edge in (2.5 cm) at the base of about 1-1 1/2 channel. Another design of 01/02 in the opening (2.5 to 5.1 cm) above the shapes of the bag directly below the channel, so that the water-continuous reuse.

• You can run on the possibility of a cylinder between the canal and even the cover, what you need is not required.

7. Advance water siphon tube at the top of its channel end. Using a drill, a saw, or the opening of a hole in the center (1.3 cm) in the focal point of the lens channel tertiary make. The finished feed roller 2-3 (5.1 to 7.6 cm) in the direction that it remains secure.

• You can also an opening at the top of its channel in the way that you prefer not to stand aside.

• The size of the gap of the tube may depend on the thickness.

Fill the pots eighth with growth medium and seeds. By application of growth of hydroponic culture medium housing, for example, perlite, coconut fiber, or vermiculite. Fill each pot so that they fully 75% before planting seeds. Then, each seed is added to 1/4 to 1/2 inch (0.64 to 1.27 cm) deep in the pot.

• Hydroponic gardening works best for fresh green grass or green.

9. Close the water trap, which runs continuously. That the arrangement siphon water to move nutrients through the channel base to make sure without spilling. The arrangement will flow through the channel and to provide the basics of their investments consistent nutrients before falling into the deposit.

• The nutrient film system always redirects a thin layer of water so that your plants grow through the channel to rootless.

• Nutrient film systems the various water plants consider to build and recycled to reduce waste, but as needed or siphon plants, the continuous leg can stretch.

• Connect leads the siphon in a programmed clock, every 2-3 hours in the possibility that it is not necessary to operate consistently siphon.

Tip: Plant roots can grow long enough to plug the channel or decline. Check that everything is going to make your channel at least once a week, always right.

Cycle operation and maintenance

Maintaining a hydroponic system

Clean water!

Tidying the room before culture. Similarly, returning before the establishment of the system and to the cultural area, clean the floor box with a provision of 10% burns. Continuous cut dead leaves and remove the culture hall. The issue of natural decomposition attracts the growth of mosquitoes. You also need to remove diseased plants, so do not spread the disease. By the time the water is changed in your deposit, rinse the tank thoroughly with a 10% melted arrangement. In the random stop with lots of space and flat sections, seen washing too much, especially in the way that you have had a problem with the spoils of the remote root.

Dropper

If you use a drip system, buy a few drops, so you can change dropper when a clogged. Do you clean a bowl of vinegar in your grow room and mingle clogged dripper to do so?

EBB TIDE SYSTEMS /

We propose a clock that can be set in a few laps so that a complete cycle simply soak the polar stone for 10 minutes. To maintain a strategic distance developed salt, it is that the upper water your plants recommended once a week. Using a similar his supply. Do not try Topwater running water (crippling their plants). So, make sure that you have with fairly deep depressions have a plate so that the water is drained, forming solid / Grodan sections.

PH value

• Do never below pH 5 or fleece stone damaged! PH less than 5 and a pH above 7, the plant cannot absorb the nutrients quickly.

• 1-2 hours before planting, remember to dip the stone fleece with water pH 5.5.

With her GRODAN nutrients arrangement at pH 5.5 and losing the channel • Rinse and then put on your system GRODAN.

The pH in your deposit increase during vegetative growth: a characteristic response - which means that your plant is growing!

in his bid increase, however, higher temperatures and green growth ph. So, beware ph. For most plants performance at pH 6.0 must associate

SOLUTION POWER

You can edit food and EC / pH calculate, but can be your answer small-scale mandatory nutrients or contaminated with Pythium (prey root). Random This memory contains you are ready (weakened) arrangement nutrients, it would be ideal if you (low pH) corrosive phosphoric acid or lemon juice used to lower the ph.

Economic cycle hydroponic

Cleaning the nutrients available, the importance of the parties on the practice of hydroponics is usually horrible little thought, and without the proper voltage results, significant and constant will not be achieved.

Neatness almost in the region is always a need to achieve higher growth and fewer problems with pests and diseases. Thus, the patient must quickly foliage plants and, at the same time, as the general wreck will be deleted, expelled from the area of growth, with more and clean surface residue, soil, and releases. Border traffic on the labor force in the region, not smoking, and sift the air supply in the area are other beneficial preventive measures.

Cleaning nutrient

Its gardeners should hear their nutrients completely for mediocre results growth censor. But in general, the real reason for the inability to usually the supply must be cleaned of nutrients.

Not as envisioned working the land, hydroponic nutrients arrangements for the environment, and are thus a perfect breeding ground for breeding certain types of infections (e.g., Pythium, Fusarium). To prevent entry disease, available nutrient medium, the roots (and so on). It should be cleaned regularly.

"Disinfectants operator" is intended to remain to give a mixture if broken in the nutrients that work with the aim of the entire system will be discussed each time the plants are watered. Verifiable, chlorine dioxide, sodium hypochlorite, chloramine, and are used for this reason. But has the advantage to have a monochloramine long half-life is difficult in the roots, and it is well used "natural" with the most means growth and advertisers in hydroponics.

Nutrients impersonation

The recycling of hydroponic systems, a supply of nutrients must be systematically repressed. -With them, that should be exhausted entirely by new nutrients and replaced. This is done to keep the nutrients and to adjust to prevent the development of destructive exacerbating and their salts (e.g., sodium chloride), pathogen, soil, and so on.

Winter and summer, usually dump somewhere regularly. Discharge repetition can be reduced if the precipitation with or RO (rotation about the assimilation) water.

Saltwater: regular dumping (e.g., periodically) could be of crucial importance when seawater is used as synthetic compounds makeup Disturbance develops faster level / toxic rainfall - especially for choking, dry climate.

The technique of casting: the poorly planned distribution equipment can make a sad and chaotic spill in the goal of which he obliged to delay or take less time to time what you expect. To take this into account to organize the plan - or before you buy. Unfortunately, most of the system plans are not think about problems dumping. Consider the benefits of the outline of the support plan:

1. Divert to waste of nutrients Insert valve line-way between the outputs and the siphon flow of the river.

2. In a perfect world, the structure of a sloped floor in the tank, which led into a tank where the nutrient is depleted. This will help remove the last liter contains only the top slag. Another technique may be less confusing to tilt the container to the outlet.

3. Sink siphons are beneficial for the ozone tank. It is lightweight, comfortable, and easy to Greenwich; However, they are exhausted usually only to a depth of about 1 inch. A low tendency deposit or implied sink for the best results is needed now.

Where discharge: Do so on the advantage of staying healthy environment in your garden or an application on a vast prairie region, and. Do not try to put chains, bathroom or in the channels or sand filling, since this could cause ecological damage (e.g., green flower growth).

Redness of the root zone with fresh water

Hydroponic systems must be eliminated in a uniform and clean manner with fresh water. (Note also that the control state of outdoor equipment is spotless just as crucial as in the tanks/channels). This is done to the development of excessive amounts of calcium (white ANIMA - causing blocking) to evacuate and unwanted/unsafe salt (e.g., sodium chloride), root exudates, green growth, pathogens, and so on the other parts of the root zone system, medium and large.

In particular, the redness of the root zone and the power supply circuit considered. Also, checks the channels, inlets, and outlets, and so on before the system charging with nutrients because they are removed during the washing process strong tendency to hindered solid material.

Courses reuse systems: The cleaning is done quickly after each dumping cycle performed. Firstly, an essential manual cleaning, for example, selling a remarkable development, and so on. To fill halfway with the supply of fresh water. At this time, the operation of the siphon with the point of the zone wash supply circuit and root/media (washing can be reinforced with a garden hose through a shower). Waste dumping removes application strategies. Repeat until the effluent water is clear, and the conductivity is in the area, that the reconstruction of the water.

Rushing squanders systems: generally, although it is essential to flush some specialists that every 7-14 days, some commercial producers think that it is flush for the day-to-day important to us! Recurrence ultimately depends on salinity, temperature, environment, plants, and the full range of variables.

Hunting techniques are:

If a) can be booked washing occurs if the nutrient tank vacancies (e.g., between clusters of nutrients), at that time, the team can be used in the current system. This is generally lower recognizable as the work of the EC type low alkalinity * to the store and nutrient casework to runoff or no more than ~ 0.5 mms, that the water in the tank. When opened quickly out of the center, it tends a garden hose to wash further advantage.

* Reduction of the pH value of tap water to ~ 5.0. RO or rainwater should not be changed.

b) If the washing is to be systematically addressed in the previous situation, at this time, a similar system is applied. However, it is vital to have a dedicated repository and siphon for washing.

This may be connected in a crossing with the supply circuit 2-way controlled by a valve. This valve is primarily directed to this repository download occurs flush everywhere.

News for neat.

two separate strategies for safety equipment required replanting is perfect above:

disease prevention

Towards the end of each harvest, it is crucial to each other hydroponic system to prevent help disinfect disease problems in the next performance. The wizard help accompanies the natural development expel pathogens, green growth, sludge, and materials / dead plants red:

Step 1. Evacuate all plants and the media, but this time many manual cleanings could reasonably expect. The outside is also crucial as neatness inside.

Step 2. partially fills the system with water. She is lowering the pH of the water to less than 5, currently with light braking conditions, including the family of the unit Bleach ** (50 g / l chloride) in about 5 ml per liter (4 teaspoonful gallon).

Step 3. Mix well so that the points system for 24-72 hours soaking. (Note that the bleaching generally strong green growth chlorine or equipment will not break.

Wet alone evacuate impurities brush) suitable for integrated processing time.:

√System Restore dogs lead the siphon at least 15 minutes continuously.

√Hurry systems to waste, the case for a short burst executed once consistently.

Step 4. Later, with this arrangement, at this stage, the whole system several times with small amounts of water to remove any brittle chlorine key ejecta to remove, and so on.

Step 5. If fine spray, drops, etc. are used to disassemble and clean independently, each unit is critical.

Anime Distance

Overall, it is even valuable time to conduct a flush acid ** to accelerate Expel (calcium sulfate and phosphate white Hasten, with running water or a wet brush cannot be solved.

Step 1. First, the system treats as the core of the question of "disease off."

Step 2: To the tank, water, and corrosive hydrochloric acid is sufficiently contained to pH 2 for example, when rainwater or RO, 30% (for example, a typical enterprise quality) lower of about a thousand overlays, or 1 ml per liter (3/4 teaspoon per gallon).

Step 3 splash system for 24-72 hours. appropriate strategies may include:

√flow at least 15 minutes for systems running again as before the siphon.

√In the race to squander siphon management systems for a burst of time and consistent Collect release.

Step 4. Then kill Available at pH 5-6 with soda waste before disposal.

Step 5. Rinse the entire system of double delicate water all corrosive keys to remove, distributed, and so on.

Step 6: When thin, sprays, drops, etc. are used, could for jumping and cleans each unit independently be of importance.

Follow the safety instructions and essential contact with metal parts.

Best plant grows

Surveys known hydroponic gardeners learning is "what had to be able to grow? Is "The basic answer is that given the available nutrients, and equalization hydroponic plants can become.

To collect the plants would be best suited for your source system, you should think about the components of this kind accompanied by the system you want or do, how much space you have, the amount of experience he has, and picking purposes behind hydroponics.

Hydroponics or technology for plants in the growth of the water can be rich in nutrients from the soil used. Still, to develop a wide range of vegetables, herbs, and various plants, some plants are better able to this dirt growth strategy without the other. Below we have analyzed ten nutritious vegetables, herbs, and fruit plants to the most natural hydroponic plants are grown at home. Similarly, these plants are adapted to technical progress aquaponics hydroponics that binds to aquaculture (breeding of marine animals such as fish) with regular hydroponics.

1. spinach

The medical benefits of green spinach make this green vegetable incredible expansion of almost all stable food systems. Still, spinach is unpretentious, well, at this point in the summary of the best plants can grow hydroponically at home.

Besides the fact that grows spinach in most water-based gardens. You can group your spinach hydroponically developed simultaneously or cut a piece at a time.

The young leaves of spinach plants cause a particularly flexible installation because it can be eaten both raw and cooked as.

2. salad

Salad's decision could probably be better maturation hydroponic gardeners known. It is slightly less difficult to grow, and you can pick the outer leaves to continue as the plant grows and the benefit of an inventory of fresh lettuce nonstop importance. I do not know what to choose the assortment? Romaine tries his additional or different, usually green, for example, Bibb.

3. cress

As the name suggests, cress is a self-esteem water system, an ideal candidate for garden hydroponics or hydroponics. It is also grown an amazing plant at home because it is not well-kept cutting, which faded effectively regulate in supermarkets contains for the cress.

This semi-amphibious plant flowers best in slightly alkaline water, and moves on.

4 cherry tomatoes

Cherry tomatoes are one of the green vegetables do not grow directly from the house at home, and in hydroponic systems. However, remember that plants, including cherry tomatoes, need a lot of light to grow, so there must be a light-independent growth or a culture cherry tomato unit with LED lamps.

5. cucumber

The cucumber plant is another case of food, the creation of a plant that grows well in a hydroponic environment or hydroponics because there is enough sunlight or the wrong light plant gets support adult. In plants, cucumber vines, remember that as they grow plants, vines, probably confirmed by a large wire mesh or childbirth. There is no room for the vines and an extensive network? Mainstream gardeners specialized species of shrubs are buying smaller than most typical types of cluster vine, and you can gently seed of cucumbers bush.

6. Peppers

are at the same tomatoes and cucumbers, peppers usually slightly inside to grow at home, and they get a ton of light or regulate their patchy growth light is amplified. Also suitable for hydroponic development. When you create your hydroponic garden at home rather than in a large greenhouse, should stew of beans and peppers other smaller the pepper assortment qualifies for small spaces sounded peppers to decide was considered.

7. Kale

Recently, medical Savoy advantages you get a ton considering the possibilities and cookbooks on flowering kale plans concentrated. However, kale is so new, but not as readily available as many different vegetables and cultivated regularly artificially carbon contaminated with pesticides. With the growth of own kale hydroponics or aquaponics or only with the ground as the culture medium, kale has quickly accessible again. On the other hand, if you grow your cabbage in a hydroponic system with controlled inside, you probably will not pesticides such as insect decimate plants need who live on the ground or fly difficulties

8. strawberries

Suppose you could have new, fruits privately grown indoors all year round! With a well-structured hydroponic system, the whole development of berries years turns out to be simple. To begin, start buying strawberries Sprinter to save a garden and in the refrigerator for two to three months before planting them into your hydroponic garden. This incentive, the process can start growing fresh hops, and his strawberry plants should flower begin after planting to deliver directly.

9. Mint

Although usually in the countryside, orange mint (also called mint water) is grown a semi-amphibious plant in nature, it is best in deep waters little flourishes on the shores of lakes and rivers. Also, orange mint, support, and a combination of spearmint and peppermint, like water. It is therefore not surprising that the two kinds of grass are some mint orange and mint aquaponic ally grow best in hydroponics or if you have no knowledge relating to hydroponic gardening. Aero Garden sells packages of garden herbs that are perfect for indoor use and are ideal for herbs such as mint, basil, parsley, and cilantro grow at home.

10. basil

Basil is another case of an herb less difficult to grow in a matter of hydroponic system. The easiest way to start basil in a hydroponic system buys basil plants in a garden square, young plants hydroponic specialist after washing thoroughly growing the dirt from the roots.

The benefits of hydroponic vegetables at home

If you go to the supermarket, you tend to have to be to buy, forced what they have? Of course, you can go to a farmer's market and a part of the application of high-street shops shopping around. In any case, what it is to be reasonable, you have the option to do so? Especially if they have a family and work, not to be as honest enough hours in the day, as we should be.

We must give high quality, dependable food for ourselves and our family. We grow, you acknowledge that you eat, and recognizes what was used to support the plant that led to the table. If you are a regular gardener that the plants in a state of growing the idea can come, it is a fake domain. I felt the equivalent until I explore some did.

The vegetables grown hydroponically has an equivalent level of nutrients, such as developed in soil. This is subject to the type of food you put more in your water. However, the equivalent of the ground can be said. Random what is called a plant grows in poor soil, it will be deficient in the remote possibility is increasing year by any means.

The support that you will get from it is also reduced. (Of course, vegetables grown in nutrients can also be changed.)

Here is a summary of some of the benefits of hydroponic plants:

• Do you know where your food comes from?

• You can avoid using pesticides.

• Hydroponic plants grow grown in the ground faster than most of the time.

• Yields are regularly more remarkable than the adult in the soil.

• Not having a garden area much room disturbing, far from the imagination of plants to grow.

Attract large plants in hydroponic fewer pests and diseases •.

• There are no weeds to pull.

• Parts hydroponic garden water.

Support tips for the growth of plants in the interior

Here are some additional tips and contemplation to consider hydroponics for your new garden:

• Lighting: Only since a plant is grown in water does not mean it does not require daylight. Especially because fruits and vegetables such as tomatoes and most anything with flowers, you have put your plants, or near a window on the southern edge, is pointless or another way to get the intense light, a perfect world, at least six hours a day. Unfortunately, this can be confusing because of the different light areas because of the strength and power to the diverse needs of different plants.

• pH: Depending on what you are trying to grow the ideal pH value of the water and cannot have the capacity of its plants significantly, ingest reduce nutrients strengths and different nutrients. (For example, mentions the above herbs above in bold pH is lower than in most of the faucet.) It is an excellent pH inclination to stop improve their plants and change the water as needed.

• Air/temperature: Like most plants tend to a temperature between 60-80 ° C, and it is remarkable how to keep hot or cold, it is around the hydroponic garden. In some cases, you must protect it from the generated heat from the lights or the coolness magnification close.

On several occasions, you need to protect against falling winter temperatures, even though they are on the inside.

What is the nutrient film technique (CLS)?

The process of the nutrient film hydroponic system (CLS) is plunged into operation in the water, the nutrient soaked in a culture dish so that the nutrients of the plant can be taken as the water through the foundations. The water is then exhausted. A lower tank is bled again by the growth zone at the end.

It is one of the most popular and flexible systems for hydroponic. It can be useful for the development of plants unusually, the light, however, has been so successful for more massive crops such as tomatoes soon as a salad.

CHAPTER 3:

Nutrition Plants, Seeds, Cut And Maintenance

Nutrients are one of the foundations of a hydroponic system. Consolidated manure together in a hydroponics system, it must be solvent. Otherwise, the system cannot reach. With hydroponics, the manufacturer of general supervision over the implementation of fertilizer in the type and attachment has. But they can quickly identify and maintain relative consistency was a nutrient meter is available. The supply of nutrients is important, and more than a dozen components to grow a plant. I added carbon, hydrogen, and oxygen from the air and water.

The other components, namely minerals, are broken in the nutrient supply and must be in the correct proportions. Any large hydroponic should contain these components; Nitrogen (N), potassium (K), phosphorus (P), calcium (Ca), magnesium (Mg), sulfur (S), iron (Fe), manganese (Mn), copper (Cu), zinc (Zn), molybdenum (Mo), boron (B), chlorine (Cl). Usually, this is with all shop's nutrients detailed pre-hydroponics. It can often Prefabricated these nutrients are available in 1, 2, 3, or more "parts" so that the manufacturer, the ratio of metallic components change either vegetative or seed and growth of the flower or to account for different yields.

Make sure to use nutrients for hydroponics at a hydroponic system. Creating components for soil nutrients is entirely different; the head of these components has grown the dust of the hydroponic because plants reach the ground. With hydroponics, no soil for parts, the two are entirely different in structure since they are not intended for plant nutrition finished and cannot soluble in water. For example, urea nitrogen is not easily accessible for hydroponic plant urea nonsolvent. And nitrogen needs in hydroponics in the nitrate structure are transported for use.

One thing that is often overlooked for the nutrient temperature is the available nutrients. The bases of the plants grow under the ground in nature and copying than they would in the environment, it is essential to keep the root zone at 68-72 degrees. This does not mean that when the temperature of the nutrient run 73 or 74, the plants of the bucket. However, it should be as possible closer to 68 to 72 degrees. Plants with high nutrient flirting can also have problems, including yellow (without limitation) flowers and fall off damaged fruit, and a lack of new growth.

Hydroponic nutrients can be an insurmountable problem, or a base, that the mixing and casting. Who inexperienced with hydroponic nutrients should only primarily a decent production and outdated inventory of carriers remain with a proven equation?

This will familiarize you with the basics of hydroponics to test before.

CHAPTER 4:

Bio Pest for Hydroponics

Natural garden pest by standard methods ...

B y a long shot, the best (and greenest) approach against the parasites in a hydroponic garden uses biological controls (beneficial predators). This is a reliable technique kindergarten and is used in the intended environment or on the patio in your home. However, for obvious reasons, you do not want 1,500 ladybugs in the room before doing!

If robbers clean your terrible mistake system, which usually disappears from the garden, there is nothing for them to eat, either cease to exist or to go in search of greener pastures!

Currently does not reject this great too confusing or expensive system. It is quite easy if you the best contact possible robbers your specific pest invasion. Demand is the electronic error of almost any garden or hydraulic power to the site easily accessible. Also, you treat your aggression without synthetic mixtures, the use of your weapons to save Mother Nature "good bugs."

These are safe for insects profit you consumed, animals, or plants. They eat only pests and their descendants.

Top 6 plant pests

They are to be parasites and how painful to the brain now ...

1. aphids with small groups of susceptible insects, soft body the mysterious underside of the leaves.

2. whiteflies were waving millions and millions of white butterflies in their facilities.

3. Mites Many small yellow spots rub the leaves of spider crops.

4. Gob masses of cotton 4. criminals' mealybugs-GOT bars.

5. Thrips are fixed part of their leaves with torsional and whitish spots or bright colors.

6. MUSHROOMS mosquitoes are swarms of fly's dark on its derivatives modest nutrient tank or the choice of the media.

There are various torments in addition to the errors that ruin your new garden. Learn more about diseases of known plants, and how to prevent and treat here:

FORMA, mold, fungi, viruses, and algae

Pest listed above

Fight against aphids

Damage to plants

The plants may look faded and destroyed, and thrive neglect. The leaves may be mottled or yellowish, becoming dark and twisted. Aphids suck plant juices in the leaves and can kill the entire plant. Aphid saliva for plants and aphid's disease infections can also transmit deadly as their hosts. Also, prevent control aphids that the spread of this dreaded disease.

APPEARANCE REEPY Crawly

Look closely, and you will discover the thickness of the small states, insects' delicate body, usually yellowish. They meet regularly on the underside of leaves or the tips of plant growth.

You can search for a way to seep honeydew attracts ants. On the possibility of what you study ants, aphids.

TREATMENT light infestation

A sweet little (1 / 32-1 / 8 inches) from the hand of aphids and crush.

NATURAL WAR

Error woman, lacewings, and nerves mosquitoes are usually the big mistake of going for aphids.

Whiteflies CONTROL

Many were small white butterflies that swarm your garden? Whiteflies sound like I find ... ways to deal with here.

Whitefly damage plants

The leaves appear shiny with "Tau" and whitish dots or stippling on the leaves. You can -white light or find descendants and on the underside of the leaves "Libra." Whiteflies suck branches, and plants without much distance can kill. They are like tomatoes, cucumbers, peppers, and even salad.

APPEARANCE ERROR

They are a little "Butterflies" white lie seen in plants. That gently shake to the possibility of the stems are spread whiteflies in a swarm, flying around at that time, have been established. Doubling is incredibly quickly mastered until the garden.

TREATMENT light infestation

Here is a perfect trick: gently shake to the ground, and when flying flock, a vacuum cleaner sucking mouth!

Or some traps bright yellow "sticky" set, the nursery is approaching or offer garden.

NATURAL WAR

Whitefly parasites: Predatory wasps (parasitic wasps do not sting); a wasp can kill many young whiteflies; Lacewings eat less.

RED mites

Red spider bugs can take over your garden before you know it. Find ways to control here.

Mites DAMAGES ROUGE PLANT

white spots on the leaves at least yellowish. With huge notes, you can discover a network that covers the top of the plant and parasites sliding spider.

The leaves eventually dark and transmission, such as vermin plant liquids.

APPEARANCE error

On the underside of the leaves, you will discover small red pests, the size of a pinhead. See them run around and find some translucent, egg white gold bow.

TREATMENT light infestation

Will take a stab at a temperature, and viscosity increases. Spider Insect direction crisp, dry lean.

BIO WAR

Phytoseiulus common enemy (predatory mites)

mealybugs

Damage to plants

Twisted leaves, weak plants can divert a plant a massive invasion.

TREATMENT light infestation

Continuously tries to run hand and can also get the high ground. Anyway, we must be careful when searching for these insects.

BIO WAR

Cochineal insect predators (bugs) Lady Love blunders to eat.

Thrips

Small yellow spots in your garden plants? Maybe ... familiar with thrips control thrips around here.

Thrips damage control plants

The leaves are finely spotted white or yellow spots, sometimes to a bright metallic appearance ahead. You can become brittle, and dark stained feces thrips are. Look closely, and you will discover the criminals.

APPEARANCE error

Travel resembles a tiny direction to the legs (about 1/16 "long). You can also dark rooms (bug feces) can be found quickly moving insects. Hurry up and can be run to see.,

TREATMENT light infestation

Grabs the opportunity, can, and crush. Pinch and support, and you can only get the high ground.

NATURAL WAR

Encarsia (parasitic wasps); tirelessly insects; lacewings

PARASITE gnats

Damage to plants

These mosquitoes penetrate the culture medium, and their descendants eat the roots of the plant. Free energy systems, and the leaves pale. However, the plant is not happening.

APPEARANCE error

Modesto's dark or weak fly with long legs and a device for receiving, fly erratic your plants. Mosquitoes parasites like sweaty natural theme lazy - So how do you find in the culture medium and can in each case, a swarm its reservoir of nutrients.

TREATMENT light infestation

You can take a stab many small irritant Beggars absorb with an intake opening. However, this is only one permanent settlement; to try Yellow sticky traps, too.

WAR Nature

Nematode parasites or relentlessly

WAS SYNTHETIC

From in the center with cleaner insecticides or neem oil.

Go use the mosquitoes explicitly to treat the parasites, and much the food can be added to good; continue to wear with caution.

The thrips

What mites they are and what they are doing mites

To have a garden responds within winter long for amateur gardening, make sure that they have their power supply. And while it is possible, but the potential risk of gain can be avoided, support and strain due to noise. The potential for high yield seeds, plants Perhaps one of the most harmful pests' insects' spiders. This guide will help you to distinguish this for

Formidable enemy and throw your garden.

What is a spider parasite?

There is no explicit type of spider vermin, a physical interpretation of a thing could be misleading to give 1200 species of the family. However, this is not a standard format that can be applied. Spider parasites are surprisingly low, mm in the range of 1 or less.

Usually, the parasitic spider is having a reddish hue; however, maybe that moves. The shape of the body is the body connection to the spider-shaped legs (hence the name). Because they have eight legs, they are not considered as an unpleasant tingling into consideration the regular 6 or less.

Because of the small body of the insect, are challenging to detect, as a rule, was flooded to the plant. One day by chance, a mistake can put Spider to 20 eggs, which can start from each of them as little as 5 days.

While you can use insect repellent to be flexible on pesticides to try to vermin because of multiplication to run a rapid, agile adaptation of species because it has the impregnation could be more enthusiastic than expected.

What are the parts of a commonly affected by mites' plant?

The petite size of the spider insects, it challenging to recognize a houseplant. Along these lines, looking for signs that your system may be contaminated, is critical. If your houseplants seem to have an opaque shade or the brightness of the plant is gone, it is an acceptable marker that something is wrong.

Check to see the underside of the leaves if the plant does not reddish spots or black temple has because they may be groups of insect's spiders. Also, the possibility that the belts are found, although it is very close to a definitive reference to the invasion Mite.

If you agree that your plant spider error, please look at the association of the steam leaves. If a small number, which can be found here or on the underside of the leaves sometimes. But because of the way he repeated very quickly, a spider that is on the side of the base of the leaf's experts in the extended discovery.

Again, check the bands and spots on the floor of the plant. But only that perception has discovered the possibility of no evidence, you can take a blank sheet of paper and gently the leaves of the plant butt pat. On the chance that your plant spider bugs at this time, must be seen in the white paper. They usually appear as pepper and (depending on the degree of invasion), appear to move.

The expectation of getting spider mites

The primary source of indoor gardeners gets spider insects on plant plants interspersed with houseplants outside. To your houseplants get the spider bugs, an important principle is not to recognize the blessing of the plants.

Although plants can be given on authenticity, it is doubtful to decide whether it is surrounded by the plant (at least that is estimated to take this opportunity in front of them). Also, because of the spider Insectile, clear whether a critical test performed at the factory, which was given as a blessing, was able to show the signs of a possible invasion.

Take bring customers to use caution and avoid outdoor plants indoors if you see a plant or shower with reasonable insects or isolate that unwanted noise accompanied primarily elsewhere until you are sure.

The removal of spider

Even with the preventive measures, it is still very profitable for a plant for spider pests. If you have recognized the problem at this time, you must fast. There are several ways you can do it.

• Use insect repellent on your system. Remember, however, that the spider bugs mimic a fast pace and are incredibly versatile. Have for the treatment of the plant and not parasites; they could be that the high toxin reached. At that time, he would have to find a different technique. Do not try to put your site directly from the factory with a very responsible insecticide cleaner that you are running the system in this way or damaged.

• Consider using miticides. These acaricides are for indoor use on certain items available, but you must make sure that you buy the right kind. Even with a registered backup, the product has an abundance of ventilation.

Again, it is possible that parasites strong or syringes, especially given the possibility that the mark already in use on the ground only.

These are not techniques for removing natural spider insects. Reduce dependence on these substances as a gardener repellent. Also, the judgment will show that when there is a logical strategy to eliminate pests, the best and most generous benefits.

How does one get rid of live mites?

To get rid of natural spider pests, you must first perform the steps described above for the detection and the treatment less (with paper and water). If you follow these key steps to continue support:

1. Ejection any sheet violent or dead plants swarms and throw them into a plastic bag. Think to seek it for the fallen leaves of the plant. If you are not connected, today, a herd accident spider can be.

2. Citrus extract: It is with oil from citrus with a base extracted parasite explicitly two or destroys three elements. If you are, when all other options have been exhausted, you cannot your own, but do it is not as profitable, always responsible place. Mixture substantially coffee powder three tablespoons extract per liter of water and shower installations, mainly the underside of the leaves that satisfy the rule.

3. Showering the use of essential oils of rosemary plants entirely. Rosemary does not harm the plant or other valuable parasites for your plant. So significant a fundamental natural rosemary oil as a "fake" that the plant could be harmful.

4. You can also use ladybugs on plants. Ladybugs feed on spiders' insects. The problem is that he could issue a question for another. Women tend to imitate insects quickly and are also

generally found its way into the windows of the stills, rooms, and other superior rooms niches and crannies. You can even bite so before it is one of the failures of a spider to test how it includes the decision to woman.

5. Pickling Alcohol: mixture as a washing section alcohol portion two and water shower on. This is probably one of the most reasonable and substantial non-hazardous and kills contact arrangements.

Only an expression of authenticity in the treatment of mites naturally. When people ask me, "XYZ murdered parasitic element? "State I:" Verily, I must slaughter a time a lot of time with him! "The fact is that there is no appeal annihilate turned. It depends on the size of the inner garden area that could be a recognizable place for you. These natural things are simply stored control techniques, a standard treatment to carry out, or go back.

The damage and decide whether investors.

If the management of spider mites, especially the keys continuous supply, which must have a non-sided mind. In all actuality, however, you have a lot of energy and money in the development of plants that invested when the plant is a danger to the rest of your diet, then that should be eliminated.

This does not mean that you go to the landfill, but you must be away from any place where the invasion could spread.

Determine the system in an opaque plastic bag contaminated and throws it away from the garden.

Keep your garden.

In general, it is a natural pest to protect freewheeling plants. In the occasion that you clean all the time your planting, spraying play to protect your investment with rosemary spiders and good luck that you (would although I was genuinely preventing wonder someone badly does) someone contaminate your garden, and overgrown plant are the odds have an amazing indoor garden, are high. Remember, their food and their resistance are at the end of his duty. Because it is a system that requires little maintenance, it does not mean that there is no support for their crops, and they will take care of you.

CHAPTER 5:

Common Mistakes And Settlement

Fundamental problems with hydroponic (and how to fix them)

Hydroponics is a fantastic way to grow plants at home that is being tested, fun, and very satisfying. However, there are some problems with hydroponically you can experience, and it is essential to find ways to maintain a strategic distance to manage these or effectively.

In hydroponics, expertise is more than growing plants in soil. Surely the ideal approach is to be taken to our confusion.

Fortunately, I grow a lot of mistakes while plants with hydroponics over the years.

1. The loss of hydroponic

Holes system can occur for several reasons. Fractures can occur at any compound or valves in the system. You can also happen if the system crashes, for example, where the root mass of TVN, the water, and overflow brings stops. The holes can even occur in the way that you can build a system with a memory that does not contain all the nutrient solution in the order. Currently, a power failure or disappointment leads the back of the place and the overflow of the offer.

solution

• Before planting, Test your order. Make sure all the valves and that all organizations are secure and tight.

Check arrested for problems such as the excessive growth of roots or channels or outlets • in your system.

• Make sure a font that selects which quietly the entire nutrient solution in the system, not just the amount that is included in it while using the system.

• If you use a cover system, be aware that on an impervious surface or perhaps a drop plate, a little remote system falls into the possibility to use. This is spilling rational thinking. However, it will also reduce disaster if to keep an eye on your system.

2. Buy, inadequate or incorrect lighting

I prefer to use my indoor hydroponic systems crunchy vegetables that can grow throughout the year. Without proper lighting of the correct type, exposure of a system will be extremely strange.

Solution

• For many people, I highly suggest a view of LED lamps and fluorescent tubes T5. These are less demanding to use and usually adequate for most customers.

• If you grow LED lights to buy, not to go for the cheaper alternative. Do some light shopping and the quality of research that provide the appropriate wavelengths of light and produce adequate amounts for your system.

• Cultural warranty purchase light enough for your system. A general guideline is to determine adequate housing area in your growing area and to increase the 65th

Here is a quick model;

A zone Increased 4 feet by 6 feet. All output area = 24 square meters.

24sqft x 65 = 1560 watts

In this zone, about 1,560 watts lighting culture growth will require. This is an ordinary general guide and is what normally associate.

3. Using the wrong fertilizer

When plants grow on the ground, they have a lot of nutrients in the miniaturized scale, now dirt in enough quantities. Therefore, compost for growing plants in the soil must not contain many small nutrients follow, which are essential for the growth of plants.

Solution

Make sure you buy nutrients for use with hydroponics.

You can add your hydroponic crap without preparation, but it is much easier to acquire a make solutions section. This can be mixed to create a nutrient solution that can be acclimated for most plants and the growth stages.

4. Do not keep things clean

On the possibility of what you leave in your hydroponic provision and environment is chaotic and confusing, it is possible to construct the risk of spreading diseases or parasites to your hydroponic system.

A part of the cleaning process is to have green growth, to stop disease and pests the opportunity to establish itself in your system. Although not explicitly systems some people use to stimulate the growth of microorganisms to work, I think it is wiser to obtain a strategic distance from pathogenic life forms for most hydroponic home arrangements, clean regularly, and the area covers your system.

Solution

• The area around your hydroponic looking for perfect and practical.

• 2-3 weeks, the channel system, flush the media and roots that grow in the water and clean business, siphons, and pipes.

5. do not learn on the fly

Each plant growing in a hydroponic system is extraordinary. Some things will work positively, so that problems, whether minor or significant. You must agree to open the door to break what has worked undoubtedly, and what went wrong, change their training for future harvests.

Solution

Recording, Photo, and watch the great and terrible parts of each system that you use and grow performance.

6. Monitor not the health of your plants

If you filter the plants regularly, you will miss the first signs of problems. Whether low growth or impairment indications or diseases that are before realizing there is a problem, the more likely you need to change and do not destroy your plants.

Solution

Detect growth and the state of its factories for the most part.

By the time you see a problem, neglecting the effort to find the problem and resolve to try.

If you observe the treatment of diseases or pests to prevent at first, and you can damage the tip of your plants.

7. Monitor and adjust the pH

The pH of the nutrient solution is critical party hydroponics. When the plants were growing in the soil, the earth as a cradle pH will prevent rapid changes in ph. This means pH problems are slow to create and manage more effectively.

This is not a hydroponic situation. The pH may be essential for hours or days varies due to several variables, including the temperature, the speed of the storage of nutrients by the plant, the proximity of the condition, the fullness of the leakage, and so on.

Solution

• A growing with hydroponics, examine the pH of the nutrient solution.

• In another system, or if there are last-minute changes have been, you may have to try to adjust the pH value change of each day. In a stable system, you can reduce the test more than once a week. The best ways for pH test with a pH meter analysis unit or a pH test. I highly recommend a meter and a half pH test of the electrical quality quickly and easily pH test.

8. nutritional deficiencies and poisoning

There are several factors that nutrient deficiency or danger in their plant's cause can. It is not easy to say in all cases, what nutrients causing the problem or defect or toxic quality is the problem.

There are signs of giving special attention to detect the deficit and lethality of various nutrients and show signs of improvement to distinguish the issues of time and experience.

pH, temperature, the growth rate of plant nutrient solution, customer error, and several different variables fixation can ruin nutrients. That excessive amounts of nutrient problems while maintaining the other may result in mind.

Solution

• A point to take a nutrient solution with care and precision.

• Make sure that the water used to compensate for the nutrient solution is not too difficult. Assuming that is the case, the weakening of the purified water or water should that was a backward path or channel carbon assimilation began to decrease the degree of the solid upward broken.

• Screen broth pooling with a PPM meters / EC

• Change the display and the pH of the nutrient solution.

Nutrient deficiency begins. • For the plant to show demonstrations or toxic quality, my recommendation is to cleanse your system, have the nutrient solution, and create a new group. Experienced breeders can have the proper equipment gradually to change things as they are. However, most beginners and advanced will be wiser to adopt a protection strategy.

9. The use of hard water in the hydroponic system

As mentioned above, the use of the chaos hard water to the hydroponic system. On the off chance that the water is less than 200 ppm, probably this can be used without severe problems. However, tap water with a significant degree of completely separated solids causes nutrient problems.

You have the option to not have the same amount of nutrients in the water to add, as they are limited by their objective approach in the nutrient solution.

Also, you probably do not know the specific determination disintegrated minerals in tap water, but if you had this secret treaty.

Large parts of hard water salts are calcium and magnesium. Unfortunately, these mixtures are generally large atoms.

Are not consumed in the location of the plants.

Huge mixtures of calcium particles in tap water can draw the water calcium salts, which can increase your plants, they cannot take to, and terrible high situation, what state of a calcium deficiency.

Solution

• If you have hard water, more remarkable than 200 ppm, which reduces to a weakening or with this refined water or use a channel, the degree of decomposition of minerals in the water.

• A carbon Channel announced the level of certain minerals would reduce and is a good alternative, modest.

• A backchannel assimilation an alternative to today's expensive, but the level of minerals will reduce bankrupt close to zero.

10. Monitoring PPM / EC / TDS

The use of a nutrient solution too low will ask the problematic plant growth. It can cause the nutrient solution to the venom of the quality or constipation nutrients concentrated. Do not wear strong plants.

Since plant assimilates nutrients and water, and water has been developed with variable rates, change the convergence of the nutrient solution. The pace of progress will be based on the plant growth rate, the same environmental conditions of growth.

Solution

• a meter PPM EC TDS Use the broth both the nutrient solution and after some time, as the plants grow the show.

• The solution can change in a certain way, if the plants do not show signs of nutrient deficiency or toxic quality.

Change the nutrient solution after a limit of 3 weeks •. This should be done as extensions of various nutrients from the beginning of the variable approach to the adoption of plants. In the case of using tap water, its broke solids that cannot be used by the plants to begin to collect.

• An EC meter has just shown that the electrical conductivity of the solution that you must do. This is changed to an estimate of the total breaking of the solids in the solution. It shows that nothing in the various segments of the solution.

Make a lot of crisp broth • 2-3 weeks prior to the possibility that evidence differs on the lethality of nutrients or failure of your plants.

11. blocked or broken pumps and spray nozzles

Hydroponic systems rely on visiting or extremely consistent transport of water and nutrients to plants. If you have a letdown or trap or lock choice, they may have trouble fast.

Rapid plants trap broken or blocked water that can be removed in many systems out of the water. Bit Systems and DWC this problem will not.

For aeroponic systems, it is very easy to inject blinded obtained for the nozzle after a while. When this happens, exposed roots dry quickly out what withered to its plants and happen quickly.

The vacuum unit can also come shortly. We need a long fall for the plant's oxygen content in the water without money to a level that the roots begin to choke, they bring in the dust.

Solution

• System time check to time.

• Consider a water or vacuum device to purchase with inherent caution that sounds when a blockage is.

• Remember to structure your system so that when a blockage or disappointment, it will not prompt the rapid disappearance of plants.

• For systems NFT method, for example, is a great way to have slightly raised the water outlet end of the channel leading into a small puddle that drain remains in case of disappointment.

12. Choosing the wrong medium culture

The decision to cultivate the media is huge, and there are many elements to consider changing the ordinance on a decision.

Some culture media are reusable, and some are only the appropriate one to use. Some are soft and keep the water around the roots of plants.

Some are vague and leave insignificant rapid filtration. Some are expensive, and some are small. Many culture media can be set to work in different hydroponic systems, and several manufacturers have their inclinations.

Solution

• Put to do aside from a touch of effort to think about what you need to the culture medium.

• Peruse reach to what others have had more success.

• Consider your financial limit, and possibly the media are reused for different harvest cycles.

13. No toilet and fill the system with enough frequency

The difficulties of growing plants can be justified with hydroponic at all, despite all the problems. Hydroponics has many advantages, such as interest and a pleasant side. However, if you try your system to run too long between washing and changing the nutrient solution, the possibility of the problems or at least the destruction will increase their income. The further you go to change is almost certain problems with illness, have parasites, and are the nutrient solution that cannot be accurately processed.

Solution

Although hydroponic much less serious than the basic gardening on the field, you need to visit more observation and change. Flush the system and change the broth a bit of a requirement is. Despite all the problems. Large products, the development of plants more quickly, and the whole year, my cooking green are to gain the benefits. Some consider the basic routine of my system is well established, despite all the problems, and how to obtain the understanding, in my ability, efficient and accurate the nutrient solution is always to change, flush the system and clean my extra memory.

14. Building an inconvenient of aquaponics

There are many things that can prolong the effort of a hydroponic system. Setting up a system in a small room without enough room to work and put it in a location that your computer is not at hand is confusing. A system that online have no water source is complaining beneficial. DIY inefficient system manufactured holes or disappointment tilt provide the motivation for their dissatisfaction.

Solution

• Bit begins. Whether it is a DIY system or a prefabricated system, it is almost no initial growth cycles should be a learning experience. If you place the terrible decisions early, you can keep moving and next plan something better time.

• Plan your hydroponic system - you need to have your computer and the water fountain near the hand and a location outside of the system, you can get prepared for a nutritious solution or clean your equipment. Random what you grow indoors, consider what could happen if there is a hole. It is his waterproof floor with water, or you can put a plate drop by drop.

15. Plant Diseases

Hydroponic plants are grown generally less susceptible to disease than plants in soil. No soil microbes and organisms are less likely to develop. In addition, the specific conditions, such as the accession wealth, high temperatures, and lack of direct light, can build significantly the risk of their investments, which means diseases that compromise the whole show.

Can perform various aspects of your system also highlights the abundance of plant stress, making them more defenseless the disease.

Solution

• To prevent disease in their hydroponic plants, you should try to maintain a strategic distance condition that pathogens develop. This includes a strategic distance from high temperatures and humidity to preserve and tried to ensure that your plants get some light quality or fake immediately.

• pH display and centralization of the nutrient solution. Make sure that the nutrient solution all plants in the basic scale and trace elements, including for their growth.

Most of the time •, your plants display no signs of the disease. In the unlikely event that you notice a problem, try to identify the cause, and treat it as soon as he could afford it.

CHAPTER 6:

Business Advise And Information On Hydroponic

Market Overview

Statistics and numbers for the past year were quite surprised that the hydroponic industry was reached at about 23.94 billion in 2018. And now, should the annual growth rate of 6 world's estimated, 8 for 2024 now of in terms of the wider market hydroponics, European countries are then governed hegemony here. You have about 47 percent of the industry in general or on the world market.

There is no doubt that Hydroponics is the clearest water-saving technology and environmentally friendly with a profitable business. Perhaps the reason it has been widely promoted by governmental and non-governmental organizations in various regions of the world. And in terms of disadvantage, then perhaps it is the high cost of the system.

But many studies and experts are working hard on this aspect.

Hydroponic scope

the hydroponic method is much easier than what we speculated. It is the work of plants through the water, the nutrient solution in gravel, sand, grow without the use of soil or ground. Today we have seen the explosion of population growth. Countries like China and India, with a population of over one billion. And for this reason, the food problem of the day. Thousands of people die every day due to lack of food.

Soils and land by day waning days due to the development model of the world. Therefore, in this case, the process or the concept can make the middle soilless hydroponic the ideal solution to the problem of soil and food.

Market trends

Today we saw a population boom. And the worst part is that 20 thousand people added each day to the list. For this reason,

The demand for food and security increased. And a continuous supply of food and resources has turned into a major global threat important for the increase in population.

States acquire a large portion of arable land or land in the name of development. And on the other hand, things like unwanted pests and plant diseases create disorder by ten worse to 16 percent per year and a terrible state.

Control of the situation and food supply to achieve the concept of hydroponics is best for us. We do not know what will happen soon, but now that is the best answer to all our questions. Maybe landless rural-urban, and rural technology develops without land, space is used and.

In the present scenario, hydroponic technology on various plants has been successfully tested and has great potential to create critical support in areas such as the Middle East, where are given millions, and millions of dollars in other countries import the body.

Tips for a hydroponic business Start

These are the business trends and the current scenario of the hydroponic industry. And let us find some tips to start a hydroponic system

1) Planning provides a model

Whether you want a restaurant or import and export. First, you need to make your model or plan to prepare for your business a success. Planning is the first step for each job because, without planning, it may not be able to carry out their actions.

So, we will know how much you want to invest in the business and hydroponic. How many systems that you want to define, type systems, business district, and many other things that can help you in the future!

2) Your business or commercial enterprise legalization

It is one of the most important aspects of any business. Can if you want to start a business, then legalized first, so you do not that to be able to steal your ideas or brand names. And of course, if that happens, that the power to prosecute or take that person in the room of his sin. In addition, legalization builds the company's credibility and trust in the brand market. Because everyone wants

To share work with glaubhaftem and legitimate business and love their capital with them.

3) taxes or make provisions

to have another important thing is that when you start a hydroponic business. And if you have the legal entity, then you should have provisions for the implementation of their respective companies. Tax provisions will help enormously if you sit at the end of the year in a chair to the countdown of the result sheet. Moreover, the tax provisions that will help you transparent with tax bodies. Can

4) Startup company account

It is important to have a separate bank account for your company business if you run a business unit. Another bank account helps transactions transparent companies in your personal account and helps to make the review.

We have seen many cases, and most of them now have an excellent example of owners suggesting a separate bank account to open for business. In addition, it will help you avoid the tax authorities of many obstacles.

5) Prepare your all licenses and permits for

hydroponic company is still new to the business, winning despite high popularity and the value of capital. And it is also related to agriculture, and the growth of related non-governmental organizations licenses only for the health of those special permits and governmental and.

On the other hand, it would be better for you if you have all the permits and legal licenses, because these are the main reasons for this are soon faced a big problem. And this can cause the permanent closure of your business.

6) GetInsured

A GetInsured is one of the most important aspects still largely the company or companies ignored. The insurance is not only useful for any company but equally important for the owner as well. Because he does not know what will happen next? And to decide for the future the best thing we can do.

She You cannot secure enough to be about your company or its future possibilities, as any misalignment can lead to close in the future

For your business. Therefore, you should get insured by a financial minimum, any incident or accident, interruption, a temporary pause, workers' compensation, and many others.

7) Go Digital

Digital platforms are the most important form of promotion, branding, advertising, and selling your business. Today, if you want to survive the brutal competition, then you must mark their presence in digital media such as Facebook, YouTube, Instagram, and many others.

Hydroponic business is relatively new compared to other pre-determined company. Therefore, you must also promote more growth and sales. And now, social networking has become the best way to discover your potential customers because every company and business houses are now on social networks.

Why Popularity get hydroponic business?

1) practice

In fact, you have the right equipment, such as hydroponics, lights, culture media, culture media, cloning trays, then it would be a very simple and convenient process for you. While there are some aspects that, if you have quite daunting little knowledge of and respect for the experience, it would be a great learning process for you.

2) stylish

if It is one of the most popular times for companies worldwide. The hydroponic market generates a value of 23.94 billion last year. So now you can imagine how popular this business sector. On the other hand, it is simply because people do not have the slightest idea of agriculture have to do research and study on the method to do.

3) effective

The world is facing a major threat to nutritional inefficiency at the time. Most of the land now appears on behalf of the development of the dream model, and the face is the inability to produce the state.

Thus, at present is the concept of hydroponic the best solution to the threat of inefficiency in nutrition and agriculture. This allows us to produce grain and vegetables with a massive growth rate. And, a little profit achieved. With the proper use of the culture medium, light,

Enough water and temperature can accelerate growth.

Summary

Therefore, they are essential business advice for those who want to start a hydroponic system. There are several reasons why hydroponic methods are gaining immense popularity and solve walking toward more inefficiency. Therefore, if you want to start a business, you need to consider these points.

Conclusion

I f you have read this far this, I can see that you start serious about your own hydroponic garden at home. Well done! You have taken the first step and the most important, get all the information you need. Now you can go ahead and start making a list of plants to grow. Then make a small list of some basic items you need to buy the home or to install and you are ready.

I also want to congratulate the right decision. The advantages of hydroponics are often used. It will help now to a healthy environment. In the first example is the use of pesticides, the component of most traditional agricultural methods is eliminated. Due to the growth of plants in a controlled room, you should not have any problem with the noise. Vegetables are fully organically grown, it that you and your family first put.

Secondly, far fewer resources are required to develop their vegetables if your hydroponic methods. The water is used for the nutrient solution recycled and reused, which means using less. No compromises occur spill that the environment and traditional gardening can harm.

Finally, Hydroponic gardening is a lot less work. He is working on a compact space and can organize all your plants at waist level, so you have on your knees do not go or rejects all the time. You will also save a lot of time.

With all these benefits in mind, I am sure it is to convince no need. So, go out and start over. Before long, you will be able to get their first harvest to harvest and enjoy your wonderful healthy harvest vegetables, full of flavor and goodness. Not only will you impress your friends with their organic products, but you can only convince their own hydroponic gardens as well as to begin, especially when they see how it easy and space-saving without chaos.

Hydroponics is difficult to cultivate a method. In fact, it is so effective, you will quickly see why people want to make the extra effort that their plants grow in this way. Is do not be intimidated by any science; in fact, if you stand on your head, hydroponic store like to give you a basic layout and clarify anything that does not receive.

If you start to get some first operating system in this way, once you get the hang, less likely to kill the monitoring a love harvest.

We hope that you have learned a lot about the main components of hydroponics and as always to obtain the best plants. The next step is the system runs to get lucky!

CPSIA information can be obtained
at www.ICGtesting.com
Printed in the USA
BVHW091444081220
595179BV00011B/1130